Ancient Secrets to

Visualizing Riches

by Alek Grigorov

Contents

Foreword

Riches are at the beginning a seed in the mind that through persistent care grows into a fruitful tree. But before we can enjoy the benefits of the mental fruits manifested into our material world, secret *knowledge* about the magical *transmutation* of our desires into tangible form *has to be acquired*, studied with great *diligence* and *put into practical use*.

The ancient Egyptians are known for their secret magical practices that were based on certain *hidden laws* that *govern the universe* and the *truth seekers* for centuries have fervently sought and *studied these laws* and their practical applications that *enriched their lives*. Such secret knowledge does exist and for those who *truly want to live an abundant life great determination, desire and faith are required* in order to learn and successfully apply what the ancient Egyptians referred to as 'heka', or better known to us as 'magic'.

Successful, powerful and rich people from different Ages do have plenty in common, but importantly they all have learned and applied secret knowledge that their contemporaries were not aware even existed. Some have used their intuitive powers to guide them to success while others have sought, found, studied and applied certain hidden from the masses principles that have helped them *manifest* their *heart's desires* into reality. And while what happens in the mind of rich and successful people cannot be seen, the results of their *mental efforts* when *directed to a definite goal* cannot be disputed for they are very much real and can easily be seen.

So dare to leave prejudice behind and open your mind to the knowledge that has made so many rich and that is meant to be used by all who *want to live an abundant life* for **abundance is everywhere and for everyone**. Learn how to *attract it* properly and **your wishes will come true!**

A.G.

A Farmer in Need

Chuma was a 21 year old peasant who was head over heels in debt. His family had been farmers for generations and all he ever knew was how to how to look after the small piece of land he had inherited from his father and how to grow wheat on it. However, he had lost the favor of the Gods (or so he thought) since his last two wheat crops were severely damaged by heavy rain and by swarms of grasshoppers. Thus he had no other choice but to borrow money to support his family and soon found himself with a heavy weight of debt on his shoulders. With each passing day his worries grew bigger and bigger, his face revealed the deep fear that was taking hold of him like an enormous snake that was slowly but surely strangling the life out of him. He would lay awake in bed for hours without end tortured by the thoughts of the inevitable dire consequences that were to befall on his whole family. He would even secretly cry so that his wife would not see the desperation pouring out of him. Quite often he would wake up in the middle of the night drenched in his own cold sweat and he would stare at the ceiling of his home endlessly thinking whether he should be thankful to the Gods it was only a terrifying nightmare that had ended when he opened his eyes or whether he should curse his ill faith for the worse nightmare was unraveling continuously in front of his tired and frightened eyes.

One day Chuma's troubles got even worse-the master of slaves who had borrowed him money came directly to his house threatening with a malicious grin on his greedy face and a sharp dagger in his hand pressing tightly the blade against Chuma's throat.

'You have 30 days to come up with the money or everything that you hold dear will become mine', said the slave owner and left.

At that very moment Chuma felt like a defenseless worm that was about to be squashed by the sole of a relentless debt collector. But he suddenly felt his whole fear transformed into a fire of anger- he became so mad with anger that he *decided* right there and then that he would *do something* to *change* his fate and that of his family. He did not know just what he had to do exactly, but he was utterly *determined to act.*

The rest of the day he spent roaming the streets of the big city, his mind enwrapped in a haze that left no memory of the past few hours. Suddenly, he found himself in front of a large luxurious house-his legs had led him to the estate of one of the wealthiest nobles called Thutmose. Chuma had previously heard on many occasions rumors about this legendary nobleman who almost everybody envied, but who was highly respected by all for his generosity and wisdom. Nobody really knew, however, exactly how Thutmose had become so wealthy and powerful, but this unsuspecting honest farmer Chuma was soon about to find out and thus have his *life dramatically changed* for the better, because of *learning* the Secret.

Chuma was so desperate that *he firmly made up his mind* that one way or another he was going to get money from this nobleman-even if he had to work the lowest of the low jobs just so that he could keep the family farm and his loved ones away from the clutches of the master of slaves. With *firm resolve* Chuma knocked on the gates of the estate and declared to the guard that he insisted on seeing the man of the house. The guard, at first, threatened to beat up Chuma if he did not leave at once, but the desperate farmer was not going to take no for an answer and started to shout that he demanded to see Thutmose. The guard was fed up with the whole situation and was just about to put a severe beating on the man, when suddenly Thutmose, who had observed the whole charade from one of the balconies of his home, came out of the house and walked towards the gates. Chuma was dumbfounded by the glory of the nobleman, whose clothing and air of confidence resembled those of the pharaoh himself. Chuma immediately knelt down to show his respect for this wealthy man, the encounter with whom would very soon *change* the farmer's destiny.

'O, noble one, please forgive my impudence-my name is Chuma and I am your slave to command', quickly uttered the kneeling farmer not even daring to look Thutmose directly in the eye. Thutmose smiled with sincerity and said 'You have my attention since your name means 'wealthy', but if you do not look at me soon you will lose it.'

Chuma replied respectfully 'It is an honor and privilege to meet you. I hereby promise to loyally serve your every need.'

'And what exactly are you afraid to ask to receive in return for your services?' wittily and scrutinizingly remarked Thutmose.

'I beg of you to allow me to serve you in whatever way you deem suitable for your daily needs. I only kindly request that you help me pay up the debt that is hanging over my head and over the heads of my family.'

'Let me ask you-if you were in my shoes and someone you have never before seen in your life knelt before you and asked for money would you even consider giving money to this awkward stranger?' replied Thutmose.

Chuma felt utterly ashamed at hearing the nobleman's question to the point that his whole face turned red. He felt lost like a sheep that had wandered off from the heard and knew not how to find its way to the heard. Seeing and sensing the farmer's desperation surfacing, Thutmose quickly ended the peasant's suffering: 'Now be honest with me young man-what is this all about?'

A Powerful Mind Shift

After Chuma explained to Thutmose how he had allowed himself to fall into the debt trap, he asked the wise nobleman for an advice on how to get himself and his family out of the deep financial hole they were in.

'*Listen* to me *carefully*! Before I can consider helping you there is a very important question you need to answer: Are you *willing* to put aside your whole farmer and family duties for the next 30 days and *carefully listen* to every word I say *and do* as I ask of you *with full faith* in my words?'

Chuma was very surprised at hearing the question and hesitated for a while with his eyes becoming blank. His whole life and the lives of his family members were on the line and knowing fully well that the time period mentioned coincided with the one given to him by the slave master earlier that same day his face suddenly changed its features and *firmness* was written in every muscle of his face.

'I am, o wise one! You have my word!' declared Chuma with seriousness in his voice that clearly pleased Thutmose.

'Remember that you have given me your word and you are now obliged to listen to me with an open mind and let every word sink in just like this glass of water is absorbed by the flour. *Watch and learn carefully*!' and the wise man poured a glass of water into a bowl of flour.

'Now start preparing dough out of the mixture, because that is exactly what is happening with your mind-you have flour, *you have the right ingredients for success inside you*, but *my words will* serve as the water that will mix with the flour and *allow your mind to evolve* with time into the mind of a rich man!'

These words surprised the farmer, but he *continued* to *listen carefully* at the same time his hands were preparing the dough.

'Are you *now ready to accept and implement* the instructions that will turn the dough into bread?' the wise man asked.

Chuma was clearly confused by now-he was not sure if he was understanding the wise man correctly, but something inside of him told him to keep his mind and ears open, so he replied 'Yes, I am ready, o wise one!'

'Take this coin, go home and draw a circle around the coin on one of the walls and then fill the circle until you have a black dot on your wall at the level of your heart. Then take a chair, put it two steps from the wall, sit on it so that you are facing the black dot and start staring through the dot for **15 minutes**. Do this **3 times a day** on an empty stomach for the next **30 days**.'

Chuma agreed and he was to see the nobleman the following day when his journey to becoming a wealthy man was to continue with a powerful mind changing revelation.

The Encounter with the High Priest

Chuma did as he was told and *diligently practiced* the ritual he learned from the wise man and after breakfast he reappeared at Thutmose's home as promised. The nobleman and the peasant were enjoying the comforts of the large home when Thutmose spoke:

'All of this that is around you now, all of this luxury was just a dream at one point or another in my life. I was not always dressed in the fine clothes you see on me now; I could not always choose the food I was to eat for my meals. I will reveal the truth to you, so that you can realize that you and I are not that different, but what separates us are the things I learned and I applied that transformed me and my life.

I will tell you an interesting story that if you listen to carefully will change your life and make you wealthy over time. There was once a boy named Akins. He was a poor boy who had nothing, because he and his family were slaves. That's right, he was in the position you are so dreading, in the nightmare that ended one glorious day.

Akins's father was a farmer like yourself, but he was in the habit of wasting more than he earned. He would drink too much, eat too much, gamble too much and he would thus ruin his family's chances of living the life everyone desires. His debt would enslave not only him but also his whole family-they would become slaves.

Akins was a bright boy and at the age of 12 he would passionately become interested in learning more about the Gods and their ways. He would always carry on his neck a pendant of the left eye of the One God Thoth that served as protection for him and his whole family-a gift he had received from his grandparents. The boy's life as a slave was more than a child should have to suffer through-day in and day out he would get punished and whipped by his master for any small mistake he would make. As the child would grow, so would the bruises on his body and the determination to alter his destiny with the help of the Gods.

One beautiful sunny day he was sent to the marketplace to buy and carry fruit and vegetables and as usual he stopped for a few minutes in front of the temple of the One God they call Thoth, the God of wisdom, the God of ancient magic. He held the eye of Thoth in his hands while vehemently praying in his own way to Thoth that he would be rescued from his miserable life and in return he would *devote* himself *to* honoring and *studying* the ways of this God. And since the boy's master was drunk on that particular morning upon seeing the boy praying instead of carrying out his commands, he once again began to whip the boy. And as the boy felt the pain of the whip, his *faith became stronger and stronger* and he kept on praying with *sincere gratitude* as if his prayer had already been heard. Little did he know that the spiritual matters worked in mysterious ways he was soon about to find out.

As the blood from the whipping started to drip down the boy's back, the High Priest of the temple of Thoth came out of the temple to witness the horrible scene. Seeing the eye of Thoth in the boy's hands and his praying on his knees while being punished by his master enraged the High Priest who commanded obedience by the uttering of a single word:

'Enough!'

All of the people who had gathered around to watch the spectacle knelt immediately before the High Priest including the surprised master of slaves who started apologizing as if his life was at that moment in the hands of the High Priest and depended on this wise man's mercy.

'Your prayers have been heard boy', said the High Priest as if had read the boy's mind like an open book and he arranged that from that day on the boy would no longer be a slave, but would instead become a priest and *serve* Thoth.

The Magic of Visualization

The next few years of his life Akins devoted entirely to assisting the High Priest they called Djehuti in the rituals performed in the temple of Thoth and he thus *learned* a great deal about the magical practices that helped the priests communicate with the Gods and serve them well, for which they would be rewarded with *higher knowledge* and attainment of greater mental and spiritual *power*. The young priests at the temple would undergo special training that would enhance their mental abilities and especially their abilities to *visualize* for the High Priest taught that those who developed these unique magical practices by diligently and *persistently* following a set of ancient and secret visualizing exercises would become master communicators with the Gods and gain numerous unspoken rewards.

Akins was extremely fascinated by this training and he would *memorize* the whole set of *visualization exercises* with ease and the instructions Djehuti gave him in correctly practicing them. He was *determined* to *become a master of visualizing* so he made it his prime objective to *concentrate* fully *every single day* he practiced each visualization exercise. These special visualization exercises were kept secret for centuries and it was forbidden to write them down-they were always passed on from mouth to mouth and that is why I am giving you these exercises and I expect you to keep quiet about them but nevertheless use them for the development of your higher mind.'

Thutmose stopped the story and leaned forward and closer to his apprentice and whispered the exercises in his ear.

Preliminary Exercise. Going into the Silence.

In order to *achieve maximum efficiency* with the secret visualization exercises, the ground of the mind has to be properly prepared first. This preparation of the mind involves *relaxing the body and the mind* of the practitioner. To do so you need to find a quiet place or room where you can comfortably sit on a chair or on a pillow with your back straightened or simply lie down on the bed. Then you close your eyes and direct your eyes and inner gaze to the top of your head, that's right, your eyes *keep looking at the top* and the more you look, the more all of your muscles begin to *relax*. All of the muscles of *your face become* more *smooth* and *relaxed*, relaxed, that's right, the muscles of the *jaw relax* and the *jaw becomes loose and relaxed* and drops a little. The muscles of the *cheeks* and the *eyebrows* also become loose, *relaxed* and *heavy*, heavy, it is very enjoyable to just *let go* and *go deep*, deep into a quiet, relaxed state of body and mind, that's right, the whole body follows and all of the *muscles* of the body *become automatically* loose, *relaxed* and *heavy*. *Enjoy* the heaviness and *go even deeper* into the silence and you can even count slowly in your mind from 1 to 3 and with each count you *double the relaxation* and *go even deeper* into the silence, that's right, you begin counting slowly...1...*double the relaxation* and enjoy *deeper* comfort...2...*double the relaxation* again...3...*double* it *again* and now *you are fully relaxed*, calm and into the silence. Stay and enjoy the feeling of inner peace and quiet for a few minutes and then slowly count back from 3 to 1 and at the count of 1 you *feel calm, confident, peaceful*...3...2...1. *Practice* this preliminary exercise for the next 30 days just before you fall asleep and right after you awake and 2 hours after lunch.

First exercise. The Vision of the Triangle.

Sit in a chair, *relax* and look at the drawing of a triangle with two equal sides for about 2-3 minutes and once your *eyes* feel strained just *close* them, count inside of you from 1 to 3 and quickly and easily *go into the silence* and *see* the *triangle* in your *mind's eye* for as long as you can, then count mentally from 3 to 1, open your eyes, look at the triangle for another minute, close your eyes, count quickly from 1 to 3 and see again in your inner vision the triangle for as long as you can and when you feel ready count back from 3 to 1 and open your eyes. *Practice* this exercise for the next 4 days, 3 times a day.

Second Exercise. The Vision of Colors.

Sit in a chair, pick a color you want to *visualize*, then look at an object that has the color you have chosen, *relax* and *focus* your *eyes* on the *color* for 2-3 minutes and once your *eyes* feel strained just allow them to *close* on their own, count from 1 to 3 and quickly and easily go into the silence and see the color with your mind's eye, allow the color to expand in front of you and see it for as long as you can, then count back from 3 to 1, open your eyes, look at the color again for another minute or so, close your eyes, count from 1 to 3 and go into the silence and *see* the *color* again, let the color expand, expand in your inner vision and keep seeing it for a few moments and then see other familiar sights or objects from your past that have the same *color*, *keep seeing* different sights with the *color* for as long as you can and when you feel ready mentally count back from 3 to 1 and open your eyes. *Practice* this exercise for 6 days, 3 times a day starting from the 4th day once your work with the previous exercise has been completed and each day practice a different color. The colors you are to see are red, yellow, orange, green, and purple.

Third Exercise. The Vision of Thoth's Eye.

Sit in a chair, *relax* and look at Thoth's Left Eye for 2-3 minutes and once you feel your *eyes* strained just let them *close* automatically on their own, then count mentally from 1 to 3 and quickly and easily go into the silence and *see* the powerful *Left Eye of Thoth* and *feel* you are *protected* by the power of this mighty God of wisdom and magic and *experience* that *feeling* of being *protected* for as long as you can and then count back from 3 to 1, open your eyes, look at the Eye of Thoth again for a minute, close your eyes, count from 1 to 3 and go into the silence again and *see* this powerful *symbol* again, focus on *feeling protected* and *enhance* this *feeling* by letting it spread around your whole being. Once you are ready simply express Gratitude mentally and spiritually to the One God for his protection and wisdom and count from 3 to 1 and open your eyes. *Practice* this sacred exercise for 5 days, 3 times a day once you have diligently completed the previous exercise.

Fourth Exercise. The Vision of the Sacred Pyramid.

Sit in a chair, *relax* and look at the drawing of a pyramid for 2-3 minutes and once you feel your *eyes* strained, let them *close automatically* on their own and count from 1 to 3 and quickly and *easily* go into the silence and *see* with your *mind's eye* the *pyramid* for as long as you can, then count back from 3 to 1 open your eyes, look at the pyramid again for another minute, close your eyes, count from 1 to 3 and go into the silence and once again keep seeing the pyramid for a few minutes and then replace this image with the image of an actual sacred *pyramid*, that's right, *see it clearly* and watch it from different angles-from one side, then watch it with your mind's eye from another side, from the top, from the bottom, then evoke the *feeling* of *owe* of the power of this sacred magical place that channels spiritual energy to the Gods and *experience* this *feeling* for as long and as *intensely* as you can, then count back from 3 to 1 and open your eyes. *Practice* this sacred exercise for 6 days, 3 times a day.

Fifth Exercise. The Vision of Time Travel.

Sit in a chair or lie down in bed, *relax* your *body* and *mind*, *close* your *eyes*, turn your eyes inside looking at the top of your head and *see* through your head, count from 1 to 3 and go into the silence and travel back into the past to when you were a child and enter the *room* you slept and played in, *see* the *wall* in front of you, now *see* the *bed* you slept in and move closer to it and even sit on it, *feel* how soft or hard it feels to sit on it, look at the floor and *notice* any *details* where you are standing, then look at the furniture in your room, look up at the ceiling and once you feel ready go back to the silence and start counting slowly back from 3 to 1 and open your eyes. *Practice* this exercise for 5 days, 3 times a day.

Sixth Exercice. The Vision of the Ocean of White Light.

Sit in a chair or lie down in bed, *relax* your *body* and *mind*, close your eyes, look at the top of your head with your eyes still closed as if looking deep inside your head, count from 1 to 3 and *go deep* into the silence and *see* the Universe you are in as a Vast *Ocean* of White *Light*, vibrating with highest and purest form of energy surrounding you on all sides. There you are just you and the Universe of White Light and nothing else. *You are* in the *center* of this Magical *Ocean* of White *Light*; you are the center of this Magical Powerful Living Spiritual Energy, *feel* the *energy* surrounding you entering your whole being and filling you with the highest and purest energy, you *feel* divine *Love* entering your whole physical, mental and spiritual body and you *feel* becoming *one* with the Vast *Ocean* of White *Light* and you start *radiating* pure *Love* stronger and stronger and *stronger, feel* and know that your *radiating Love* is spreading instantly in this Infinite Ocean of White Light and now express and *feel* as *intensely* and *sincerely* as you can deep *Gratitude* for all of the positive things and people and events that you can think of, *enhance* this *feeling* of *Gratitude* to the Gods as much as you can and for as long as you can and when you are ready to return, just count slowly in your mind back from 3 to 1 and open your eyes. Practice this exercise for 5 days, 3 times a day.

Now in order that you fully *memorize* these *exercises* you have to put them to the test and start using them *daily*. Do the exercises in the exact order given-start with the preliminary then the first one for the allotted time and only then replace the first exercise with the next and so on. Go back home and for the next 30 days practice these secret rituals that will serve as the base on which *you* will *develop* a mighty house of *riches*!'

'But what about the debt? I have only 30 days until the slave master comes to take everything away from me?' replied with fear in his teary eyes Chuma.

'Cast all fear aside for it is poison to your mind. **Be Courageous! Be Determined! Have Faith!**' and Thutmose opened the gates of his mansion and showed the farmer the direction which he should be headed to by shifting his eyes.

On the way to his home Chuma was confused and fearful-on the one hand he had promised to follow the wise man's commands without hesitation, but on the other he was risking losing everything he held dear to his heart. And suddenly, amidst this perplexity and cloud of doubts hanging over his head, he remembered for some strange reason the last words Thutmose spoke to him and he repeated them in his mind: 'Cast all fear aside...**Be Courageous! Be Determined! Have Faith!**'From that moment on the shadows of his fears disappeared and it was as if his *mind* was *illumined*. He was sure he was going to put everything on the line, but he was *determined to act* as advised instead of doing nothing.

The Strangling Iron Clasp of Time

For the next 30 days Chuma was a man possessed-he followed every instruction from the wise man, he did every exercise in such a serious, *concentrated* and relentless fashion as if his life depended on it. Strangely enough with every passing day Chuma was getting more *determined*, more *focused*, his *self confidence* began to *grow* in leaps and bounds. His *mind* was *clear, efficient, poised* and *powerful.* As promised he went at the end of the 30th day to see the nobleman even though he was still unaware of what exactly to expect, of what might happen to his family or his land by the time he was in the wise man's home, but he felt very calm and ready for anything that fate had in store for him.

Upon seeing the friendly, happy smiling face of his mentor, Chuma felt as if someone had lifted a huge stone from his shoulders and thrown it to the side. He smiled back and greeted Thutmose politely and they both sat down to enjoy a light breakfast of fruit. The servants of the host had placed numerous dishes of fresh and ripe fruit before the guest, whose appearance was still very much serious and he looked as though he could not see the food that was right before him.

'I can see that you have kept your word and have *practiced* with great *commitment* and *diligence'* spoke Thutmose.

'But how did you...'

'Know? Let's just say sometimes the invisible can be seen through the visible' commented the wise man.

'I have indeed done as you asked of me, but I do not know what is to become of me or my family after my visit here. The deadline has been reached and...' began with hesitation Chuma.

'Has it really?' asked with a mischievous smile Thutmose.

'I...' Chuma was searching his mind to find a proper finish to his sentence as he was perplexed.

'You have been evolving and the so called deadline has been extended.' The wise man finished the sentence for him.

'But how?' Chuma was still trying to make sense out of these unexpected words.

'Does it really matter how?' Is it not more important that you *continue* your *journey* on the path to *riches*?'

Chuma was silent as he was looking with owe at this great man next to him and after a few moments he simply replied *'Yes.'*

'Now that we have cleared this matter up let us get back to the story of the young priest.'

Akins had *mastered* the secret *visualization* exercises and this had not gone unnoticed by the High Priest who by that time had already grown fond of this particular disciple of his who had demonstrated *interest* and *persistence* during the *studying* and *applying* of the magical practices. One day Djehuty had summoned his apprentice and looked deeply into his eyes with his piercing gaze that penetrated the being of the young man to its very soul.

'You wish to *learn* more, do you not?' asked with a chilling tone of voice the High Priest.

'Yes, o illuminated one.' answered with *great enthusiasm* and little flames of excitement in his eyes the young priest.

'You are now ready to embark on the higher plane to *learn* the higher secrets of *manifestation*, but as you know, *patience* and *self-control* have to match the higher knowledge received for otherwise you would be deluding yourself.' spoke the High Priest.

'*Practice* the following secret exercise that was passed on to the ancient Magi by the Gods after countless hours of the highest *meditation* and magical practices; from generation to generation it has been practiced only by the knowledgeable ones until the present day. From this day on your waking hours have to be devoted to practicing this one exercise constantly, *persistently*, unceasingly so it floods your mind to its deepest recesses. It is one of the most important hidden keys to always attracting the very best to you in your whole lifetime if you practice it until the day comes for your soul to leave your body and travel to higher planes of existence. *Remember* and *affirm* at all times in your mind *with great enthusiasm* and devotion the magical phrase: '**I feel Wonderful! I feel Great!**' Your success in life will very much depend on how *persistently* and *enthusiastically* you *affirm* the magical words until they become deeply engraved in your mind and being like the ancient engravings on the magical stones that will stand the test of time for millennia to come. *Remember* to use the ancient technique that maximizes the effectiveness of all you affirm: *Alter* your state of *mind* first! By now you have learned the technique of going into the silence and you can freely use it as well, however, now you are learning an even greater, more potent technique of altering your mind: *Alter* your *mind* with your *eyes* wide *open*! That's right, *defocus* your *eyes* and pay attention for a few seconds to how *calm* and *rhythmic* your *breathing* becomes as you *keep* them defocused and then *affirm* your magical words that will improve your life with great power!

The Ancient Book of Thoth

Akins started to *apply fervently* the secret ancient magic *words* that he had received from the High Priest. It became an obsession with him and he would devote himself night and day to *mastering* the magic ritual as *perfectly* as he could, he was as *persistent* as the ravenous wolf when hunting his pray. Soon enough Djehuty began to notice clearly the metamorphosis that the young priest had gone through and witnessed the tremendous evolution of the magical powers of his young apprentice. By that time the High Priest was sensing that his own time on Earth was coming to an end and needed the young priest's assistance in continuing his journey to the Field of Reeds also known as Aaru. That is why one day he called on the young priest and made him the ultimate offer.

'With the secret powers of Thoth you have evolved into an exceptionally knowledgeable and gifted priest. You have truly proven on many occasions your devotion to the One God called Thoth, you have served him well, for which you will be *highly rewarded*. You have heard of the legend about the man who was willing to go to any length to *gain* the ultimate *knowledge* contained in the Book of Thoth that is said and believed to have been written by the very hand of the One God. As legend has it this young man after a series of life threatening obstacles finally entered a sacred ancient cave where he found the Magical Book radiating an intensely bright white light. Upon opening the book the whole cave became illumined with the bright white light as if an explosion of light had taken place.'

The High Priest paused and scrutinized the face of the young apprentice. Akins's whole demeanor had *become enlightened* by what he was hearing.

'The High Priest who taught me was that young man, but he was not as open at sharing the ultimate knowledge with anyone as I am with you. However, after years of faithful service to him he did finally reveal one of the Highest Magical rituals ever known to man and I will share it with you on the condition that you help my soul continue its journey and pass successfully Duat, through the realm of the Dead, so that it reaches Aaru when the time comes.'

Akins gladly accepted the High Priest's offer by bowing politely. Then Djehuty took out an ancient magical tablet that illumined the young priest's eyes and mind instantly.

'This is what my teacher referred to as the **Ancient Magical Pyramid of Manifestation!**

The Pyramid of Manifestation

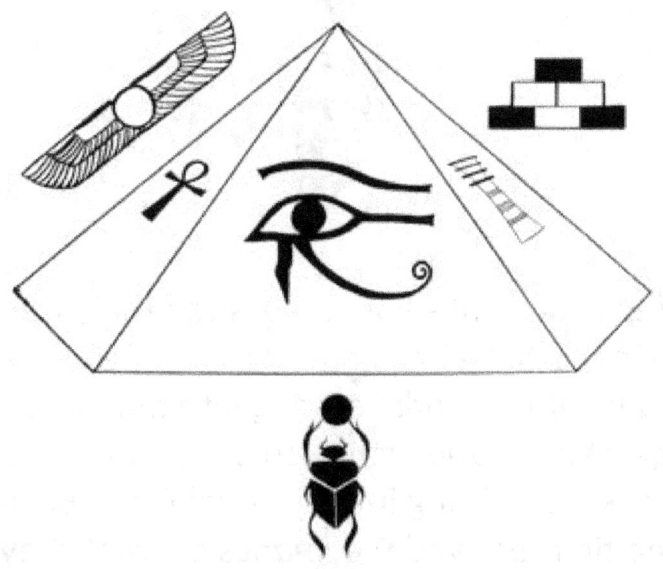

It truly contains all of the necessary secrets to manifesting one's desires provided that the hidden *knowledge* of the pyramid is known and properly and *persistently applied*. I shall now give you the ultimate keys that open the portals of the Gods that bring into material existence one's desires. *Study, visualize, memorize and apply* the magic of **the Pyramid of Manifestation** and you can have anything your soul desires. The Master Lesson begins now so *ready yourself* to *receive* the *knowledge* you have been seeking for so long!

The Master Goal

The first magical step represented by the base of the pyramid is *defining* what your **Master Goal** is to be! You have to *know with* great *precision what* it is exactly that *you want* the Gods to bring into manifestation. You need to *create a clear image of what you want*-you can go into the silence and *ask* your *heart what it desires* to bring into material form. Be like the architects of the pyramids who first *received* the *images* of what they were to bring into the material world with the help of the Gods by *allowing to be inspired* by the ideas they held dear to their hearts and by transforming these ideas in the silence into a picture that would crystallize and become clearer and clearer the more often they would search within the silence. Once *you have* the *clear image* of *what you want*, let it become the **Master Goal**, let it overpower the smaller goals and thus sit on the throne as a King to all other goals. As you give this one *definite goal* the ultimate power and title King it *becomes* the most *important* in the domain of the goals and hence its needs have to be met first, last and every single time. It should dominate all other goals and the more often you *think* and *see* your **Master Goal**, the more power you give it.

Commit to *memorizing* and easily *retrieving* this first magical step by *visualizing* the ancient powerful *symbol* of the **Sacred Scarab** holding the morning sun which represents your **Master Goal**. From now on when you *see* the *symbol* of the *Scarab* it will *automatically* be *associated* with the **Master Goal** in your mind!

Desire

The second magical step represented by one of the lateral edges of the pyramid is *feeding* constantly the *flame* of **Desire** until it *becomes a Bonfire*: This *Bonfire* of **Desire** has to *burn at all times* and in order to *keep* the *Bonfire big* and its flames rising, *you* need to *feed* it with *Strong Emotions*. And the best way to do so is to *go into the silence* and *imagine* and *feel* just how *great* it *feels* when *you have what you want*. *Concentrate* on the powerful positive *feeling* of *satisfaction* that begins to burn inside you knowing your **Master Goal** *is coming to you*. Then once you come out of the silence the flames of **Desire** will *keep burning persistently* until you get in material form your object of **Desire**. Your *want* to have in your possession *what you desire* has to match the desire of the ravenous wolf to taste the meat that will allow him to continue to live. You have to *be* like a man *possessed by* the spirits of *your* **Master Goal** that will give you a piece of mind only when *you attain* your **Grand Desire**. You have to *control your thoughts* and what you want has to be in your mind *at all times*. Keep the **Desire** whispering in your ears the rewards you are to get, the *feeling* of *satisfaction* that cannot be measured but has to be experienced to *fully appreciate*. You have to *sacrifice* all other irrelevant *small desires* on the altar of your **Grand Desire**.

The Grand Priest recommended *remembering* this step by focusing in your mind's eye on the *vision* of the powerful *symbol* of the **Winged Disc** that clearly shows how the seed of *what you want* rises to higher planes. From now on a single *glance* at the *symbol* of the **Winged Disc** will automatically *bring* into your *mind* the *Bonfire* of your **Grand Desire**.

Faith

The third magical step represented by the second lateral edge of the **Sacred Pyramid** is to *ignite* within your heart the *illuminating* **Faith** that *knows* and **Confidently Expects** that by the infinite power of the **One God** *what you desire* is being brought to you in unfathomable ways. You have to **Earnestly Believe** with the most powerful **Confidence** in the **One God**, you have to transmute your **Undoubting Hope** into a strong *radiating feeling* of **Joy** *knowing with* the utmost *certainty* that *what you* so passionately *desire you* always *attain*. You have to *go into the silence* and plunge into the *Omnipresent Universe of White Light surrounding you* on all sides and *know* and *confidently expect* that the image of your **Master Goal**, the object of your **Grand Desire**, has been 'engraved' in the Universal Mind of the **One God** and hence it *is on its way to you*! *Feel* pure **Love** and **Gratitude** with your *heart* and *know it is* done! *Know* and *confidently expect* that *what you* so deeply *desire* to have *is* on the right path to **Manifestation** and *you are* also on the right path to *attracting* it faster to you! *Let* the **One God** *infuse* you with *divine essence* and let it pervade throughout your whole being. **Be Enthusiastic**, *think* and *act* with **Enthusiasm** in your heart and *know* and *confidently expect* what you *have so persistently* wished for.

Visualize the ancient powerful *symbol* of the **Ankh**, knowing that it is your **Faith** that breathes 'Life' into your **Master Goal**, your **Grand Desire**. From now on every time you *see* the *symbol* of the **Ankh** your mind will automatically *connect* to your **Strong Faith**.

Will

The fourth magic step represented by the third lateral edge of the **Sacred Pyramid** is to *unleash* the power of the **Will**. You need to *act* with **Purposeful Determination** to *bring* into your possession *what in your mind* and in your heart *is* already *yours*.

You need to *develop* your powers of **Concentration** to the highest degree in order to assure *you are victorious* with everything you undertake that would bring you closer to achieving your **Master Goal**. The Secret Master Key to developing your Powers of **Concentration** is to *combine* **Focused Attention** with **Unceasing Curiosity** *and you* shall *have* a mighty sword that will give you *god like power*. If you feel your **Attention** losing *focus*, *increase* the **Curiosity**; if your **Curiosity** weakens, *keep* your **Attention** *focused* and *experience* the magical power of **Concentration** that will *elevate* your **Willpower** and *you* will *accomplish more* than you have ever dreamed possible.

You have to learn to *control your emotions* and use them to your advantage. Think of the wild horse-that is what emotions are; now think about the Courageous Warrior riding the wild horse into battle. If he cannot control the horse, he will meet his demise, but by *employing* **Strong Will** he *controls* the wild horse and it leads him to countless battles, it becomes his faithful ally that helps him be Victorious, win battle after battle. *Control your thoughts* and you control the wild horse, *control your breath* and you control the movement of the wild horse.

Transmute the energy of your *sexual desires into* **Willpower** and you will have learned a most powerful magic spell that will *enhance your creativity* in whatever direction you *channel it* to. *Go into the silence* and *visualize* and *feel* the *energy* of procreation *ascending* from the base of the spine *upwards* through your spine towards the *center* of your *brain* where your **Will** resides, *feel* the **Will** *commanding* the energy upwards, *feel* this vital *energy* as a powerful lightning *charging your* whole *being* as it reaches the domain of the **Will**, *experience* a most *intense* and *energizing* surge of **Power**.

Develop the *habit* of *concentrating* your renewed sense of vigor to *complete* each day the *hardest tasks first* and your **Will Power** will be as mighty as the Gods and you will *feel* and *know* in your heart that **You are always The One God's favorite**.

Develop a character of **Will**-*develop* **Self-Confidence** and **Courage** through the power of **Affirming** the secret magical seed spell **'I AM'**. The ancient magicians have known for ages that by *going into the silence* and by *affirming* **'I AM Confident! I AM Courageous!'** and *seeing yourself* in your mind's eye *as confident* and *courageous, feeling yourself* becoming *full of Confidence and Courage, you are so*! Act with **Confidence** and **Courage** *daily* as in your *visions* and you *become* a most *powerful* magician.

Fix in the *mind* this fourth magical phase by *visualizing* the **Djed pillar** and *know* in your heart that **Will** *is* the backbone of the successful magical *manifestation* and it is *making you strong* and on the side of the Gods. From now on every time you see the *symbol* of the **Djed pillar** all of the ideas of the **Power** of the **Will** will automatically flow into your mind.

Visualization

The fifth magic step represented by the lateral edge of the sacred pyramid is to **Visualize** your **Master Goal** as already *attained* and to *infuse* your *vision* with the Highest **Positive Emotions** culminating with the divine power of **Thanksgiving** for *receiving* your **Grand Desire**.

Visualization is the higher magic of *communicating* your **Heart's Desires** in the form of **Mental Pictures** *powered* by *strong positive emotions* directly *to* the *omnipresent Mind of* the **One God**! *Go into the silence, create* in your mind's eye *clear colorful mental images* of your **Master Goal** and the *attainment* of your **Grand Desire**, *focus* the power of your heart *on feeling intensely* **Joy** and **Love** *radiating from you* as a result of *receiving* your **Dream**, *sing* most *cheerfully* your *appeal to* the *Gods* and before you conclude this magic ritual, *express* in your **Heart Gratitude** for what is now yours, given to you by the Mighty Gods in their own mysterious ways.

Practice the primordial magic ritual of *condensing* your **Master Mental Creation** *onto* a *papyrus* scroll and this powerful magic tool will *increase* the *attracting* power of your **Grand Desire**. Ever since the dawn of Creation man has used this magical tool, called **'Painting the Vision'**, to *attract* to him his *strongest desires. Draw* with great care, concentration of mind, hand and positive emotion *what you* have already *created in your mind*'s eye-your **Master Goal** *attained. Draw* a *symbol* of the **One God** on the magic scroll, *add powerful words* in the picture that *stir* your *feeling* of **Joy** and *express* your **Thanksgiving** on the scroll for *having attained your wish*. Then hide the scroll, do not show it to anyone, it is only for your eyes and heart and mind. As often as you can look at the scroll and then *go into the silence* and *practice* the magic ritual of **Visualization**.

In order that you always *remember* this fifth magical step, *visualize* the **Primordial Hill** as the powerful *symbol* of **Creation** that from now on *symbolizes* the Magic Art of **Visualization**. Every time you *see* the **Primordial Hill** all of the secret knowledge about **Visualization** will be immediately known once again to your mind.

Manifestation

When you *combine* the five magic *steps*, the combined energy *becomes* so highly *concentrated* it starts to vibrate at the highest frequency and it becomes a most powerful two way *channel of communication* with the Gods. *Visualize* the *ascension of* the *energy* from each edge of the pyramid, how it is *concentrating* at the highest point and then is being *projected* in the higher dimension above. **The Master Goal** having now *evolved* into a higher form of energy has begun to sprout *in* the Universe of *Mind*; it has begun to *germinate* in the Dimension of the Gods and is coming to you! Now you have to *ready yourself* to *receive* the fruit of your magical practices.

The Magic words of hidden wisdom to live by are: **Give to Get**! You have to put your whole body, mind and soul into *acting* **Now**! *Act* to the best of your ability *in* your *present* environment. *Serve* your fellow man *as best as you can* in the conditions you are in and know your gift of *giving, serving, creating* with your labor to *fill the needs of others, adding value to other people's lives* will yield you what you have asked for! *That is the Law*!

Visualize how the divine *energy* begins to *manifest* in the middle of the pyramid. The *symbol* of **Manifestation** is the **Left Eye of Thoth**, the God of Magic, the God of Wisdom, because it is through him that you get your **Heart's Desire**. From now on every time you see the **Left Eye of Thoth** in the center of the pyramid your mind will automatically *recall* the whole secret hidden magic ritual of **Manifestation** as you now *know it in your heart to be true*!

The Magic Spell of the Pyramid of Manifestation

Now that the best kept secret has been revealed to you *commit to memory* the whole magical *ritual of manifestation* by *going into the silence* and *visualizing* the ancient sacred *pyramid and all* of the *symbols* constituting the different steps of the ritual. I repeat again the importance of *visualizing* the *energy* of the pyramid *ascending* through the edges and *concentrating* at the highest point at the top. *Visualize* that a beam of *energy* is *projected* out into the higher hidden dimension of the Gods and then the energy of *manifestation begins to form* mater in the center of the pyramid and the magical practice is now complete and *can be used* over and over again *with every* new **Master Goal** you choose to *create in* your *mind* and *heart*. To aid you in *remembering* the magical ritual of *manifestation memorize* the following *words* of wisdom as you *visualize* the *symbols* for each step to manifestation and you shall always know the highest magical secret:

'*Define and give birth to your*

Master Goal,

Let it rise on the wings of

Desire,

Breathe Life into it with

Faith,

Be Strong with the pillar of

Will,

Create on the steps of

Visualization,

And receive with

Thanksgiving

And

Service

 The

Manifestation!'

The Hidden Magic Master Key

Djehuty ended his instructions or so it seemed and was inspecting the young priest's reactions. Akins could hardly hide he was deeply fascinated by learning this great hidden secret magical ritual. However, he *kept* his *composure*, bowed down before the High Priest and *thanked* him and the Gods for *being blessed* to have *received* this privileged *knowledge*. Djehuty reminded the young priest's promise to assist him when the time would come for his soul to depart from his human body. Akins assured the High Priest he would keep his promise and it would be a great honor for him to help Djehuty at such a unique magical time and days after this conversation the Young Priest held his promise and used his magical abilities to complete the secret funerary magic practiced by the initiated ones.

But apart from that, there was only one thing on Akins's mind-to *put* the *knowledge* about the **Pyramid of Manifestation** *to* the *test* and it did not take long before he was *convinced* beyond a shadow of a doubt that the High Priest had *revealed* to him a truly unique magical *practice* that brings *results*. However, the young priest could not understand why the magical rituals of the **Pyramid of Manifestation** did not always work as he wanted them to. At times it seemed to Akins that he was missing a secret ingredient that would *complete* the **Pyramid of Manifestation** and allow its full power to be summoned to *practical use* every single time instead of only occasionally.

That is why the Young Priest went *into* the *silence* and *asked* for Thoth's *wisdom* to reveal to him if there was anything missing from the High Priest's instructions and for some reason an image of the ancient *symbol* of **Power**, **Dominion** known as the **Was** appeared in the young man's mind while still being in the silence. Akins pondered for days why he saw the **Was** and what that really meant, but he remembered what Djehuty had taught him when he was still a youth: *'He who seeks finds!'* so Akins kept going *into* the *silence* and *asked* Thoth for directions on where to find more about what the **Was** *represented*. He was led to the chambers of the already deceased High Priest and after countless hours of searching, the Young Priest finally *uncovered* the *secret* of the **Was**-inside one of Thoth's statutes was hidden a papyrus scroll with the exact *symbol* of **Power** and underneath it was written: '**Persistence**-the **Was** of the Gods that *unleashes* the high magic of the pyramid only to those who have *learned* the secret Magic of **Manifestation!**' Akins immediately remembered the High Priest teaching him the *fascinating power* of the *dripping water* that *over time wears away a stone* and it was right at that moment as if the High Priest was speaking to him even from other dimensions on the secret of this hidden **Magic Master Key**.

From that day on Akins truly had at his *command power* beyond normal comprehension. Every **Master Goal** he would *define in* his *mind* would inevitably *manifest* due to his *persistent* magical *practice* and he would *keep mastering* the magic rituals of the **Pyramid of Manifestation** to *become* a *wealthy* man.

The Revelation

Chuma was breath taken when the story of Thutmose came to an end.

'But how did you ever learn about the secret of the **Pyramid of Manifestation**? How come you *know all of the details* of the story of the Young Priest?' asked the still mesmerized farmer.

'Because I was once known by the name of Akins, but after years of devoted service to the **One God Thoth**, I was given a new spiritual name-Thutmose, which means 'born of Thoth'.

After I learned the whole secret of the **Pyramid of Manifestation** I *devoted* years of *my time* and magical abilities to *use this* high *knowledge* that I have revealed to you for *becoming wealthy*. I have always wanted to *become* better *well off* than my parents ever were and I did my very best to *concentrate all* of my *efforts* into *visualizing* a richer, more *abundant life* for myself and my family and you can see with your own eyes the wonders this magical *knowledge* has allowed me to attain through the years of *persistently applying* the secret practices. Now you see why you and I are not that different-it is the principles and exercises *I learned* and *applied* that transformed me first and then *transformed my life*.

It is amazing how fast you can *begin to attract wealth* into your life if you apply yourself the right way. **Abundance is everywhere and for everyone**. The **One God** wants you to *live a* fuller, *richer life* and you can have that dream life if you only *use the knowledge* that is now yours to use.

Secrets to Riches

'If you *want to be wealthy*, live a richer life and have the things your heart desires there are also a few very important secrets to attracting riches I learned and that have served me well' said Thutmose and he had his servants bring **10 loaves of bread** which they placed right in front of Chuma.

'This is the exact amount of bread I was paid for my services when I first *started* uncovering the *path to riches*. *Learn* this lesson well-out of every **10 loaves of bread** I was determined *to save* from **3 to 5 loaves of bread**! *Saving* can *make you wealthy*!' said Thutmose.

'But weren't you hungry with only half of what you earned?' was befuddled the farmer.

'I was hungry, but my hunger was different-I was *hungry* for a better, *richer life* more than my belly was for what I was paid at the time. Soon I *learned to invest* what I saved into other goods that *made me richer* and my life became dramatically richer.

I also *learned* that by *providing service to as many people* as *you can will enrich you* even faster and faster! Think not of how much will be your reward for your service. *Focus* like the sunlight when it goes through polished natural crystal on the magical spell you say when in the silence: '*I serve with the greatest possible* **Enthusiasm** *I can*!

And the last magical secret to attracting riches is this-*affirm* when in the silence *with* great **Enthusiasm** and **Confident Expectation**: '**I am Thankful** *for 10 times what I now have*!'

Out of Debt and into Wealth

'Your *mind* has *changed* already *a great deal* and *you are ready to manifest* your deepest *desires* and *improve* the *life* of your family. However, there is one last secret I will share with you that not many are aware of and even fewer can actually grasp fully its power and significance to *attain the dream life. Listen* carefully *and learn* this secret well: **We attract and manifest what we think about most of the time through the power of the strongest emotions we allow ourselves to feel!** Therefore, *think* only *positive thoughts, feel positive emotions with greater intensity* and always *serve with a positive mental attitude* and *you are* way ahead *on your road to success, riches and happiness.*' Thutmose concluded his teaching and looked with satisfaction into the eyes of his apprentice and put his hand on the young man's back as a sign of his friendliness.

'*I am* forever *grateful* to you and to the **One God** for the exceptional knowledge you have taught me. I will not fail and I will make you feel proud of your loyal servant and apprentice, o wise Master of the High Magic.' answered Chuma with *determination* in his whole body language.

'I know! Come tomorrow and *prepare yourself* to *employ* all of *what I have taught you* for there is much more we have to *bring into manifestation* together.' replied Thutmose.

'I am honored that you are giving me such a great opportunity. But first I need to face the slave master and his new dire demands.'

'Forget the slave master for he is in the past, he is a shadow of your former self that does no longer follow you.' answered with a smile the wise man.

'What do you mean?' asked Chuma with a puzzled facial expression.

'You no longer owe him anything. The debt has been settled! Come tomorrow and work for me!'

Chuma was dumbfounded by the words of the nobleman and as a sign of his *deep appreciation* Chuma bowed down and kissed the wise man's hand for he knew deeply in his heart that true magic was in full effect and *life is full of abundance and joy*.

From that day on Chuma *worked alongside his mentor* and *within* the next *5 years* he truly *became well off* and *lived an abundant life* by following his mentor's teachings. He *became* an *avid practitioner* of the magical steps outlined in the **Pyramid of Manifestation** and thus *changed himself first* and *attracted riches* and *happiness* into his life.

Five years after having met his mentor for the first time on the 18th day of the first month of the year Chuma and his whole family joined Thutmose and his family in celebrating the Thoth Festival that was a joyous celebration of the birth of the One God Thoth centered on rejuvenation and rebirth. Chuma had brought a well baked bread and offered his dear friend and mentor the loaf of bread by saying: 'You had already visualized my offering you this bread all those years ago when you asked me to mix the water with the dough, didn't you?'

Thutmose just laughed heartily and the two friends enjoyed together the delicious bread that was a *manifestation* of their 5 year long *collaboration in perfect harmony*.

The End

www.ingramcontent.com/pod-product-compliance
Lightning Source LLC
Chambersburg PA
CBHW081147170526
45158CB00009BA/2736